THE

GHOSTLY TALES

OF

PHILADELPHIA

Published by Arcadia Children's Books
A Division of Arcadia Publishing
Charleston, SC
www.arcadiapublishing.com

Spooky America is a trademark of Arcadia Publishing, Inc.

First published 2023

Manufactured in the United States

ISBN 978-1-4671-9739-7

Library of Congress Control Number: 2023937855

Notice: The information in this book is true and complete to the best of our knowledge. It is offered without guarantee on the part of the author or Arcadia Publishing. The author and Arcadia Publishing disclaim all liability in connection with the use of this book.

All images used courtesy of Shutterstock.com.

Spooky America

THE
GHOSTLY TALES
OF
PHILADELPHIA

BETH HESTER

Adapted from Haunted History of Philadelphia by Josh Hitchens

arcadia
CHILDREN'S BOOKS

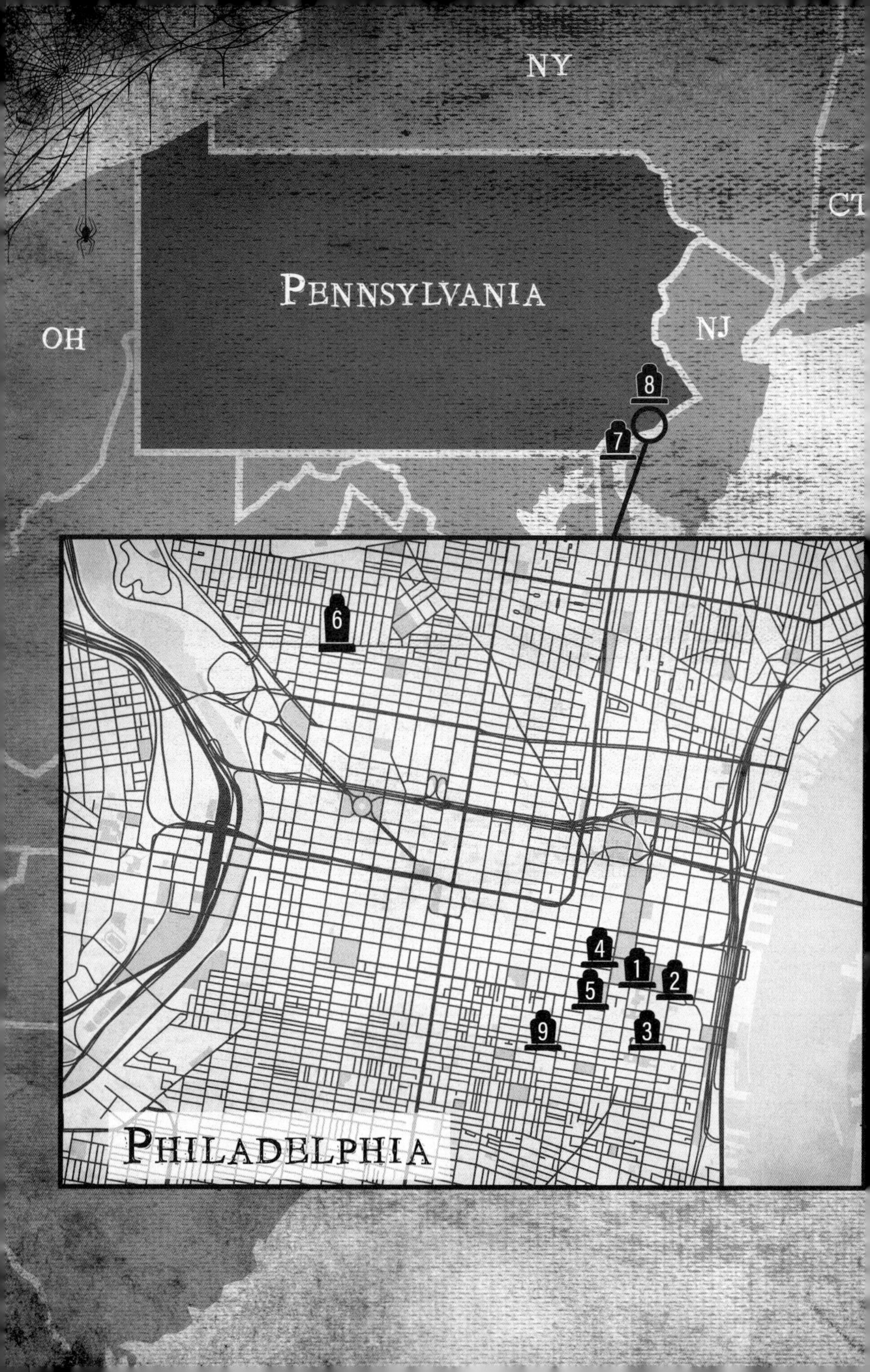

NY

CT

PENNSYLVANIA

OH

NJ

8

7

6

4
5
1
2

9
3

PHILADELPHIA

TABLE OF CONTENTS & MAP KEY

Welcome to Spooky Philadelphia!

From the first bite of a Philly cheese steak to the last inning of a Phillies baseball game, Philadelphia has lots to offer visitors and residents alike. You will certainly want to visit the rooms where the country's founders created the US Constitution and tour the historic homes of Betsy Ross and Benjamin Franklin. You may want to spot exotic animals in the zoo or stroll through world-class art museums. You'd enjoy cheering on local sports teams including the football Eagles, the 76ers basketball team, the Union soccer team, the hockey Flyers, and baseball Phillies. Philadelphians love all these highlights of their city. In fact, they love it so much, some of them never want to leave!

This book is filled with their stories: The gory and the ghostly, the spooky and the

spectral, and all those who just can't tear themselves away from the "City of Brotherly Love"—even after death. But first, let's set the scene about Pennsylvania's past.

Three centuries ago, when American colonies still answered to England's monarchy, William Penn was granted land that would later be known by his name: Pennsylvania. Penn and his companions were not the first to arrive

in the area. Swedish explorers had named this land "New Sweden" before the British took control. Before that, Dutch settlers had staked their claim. Earlier still, the peaceful Lenni Lenape tribe inhabited this land. To the English king, none of that was important now—he saw the land as his to take and give. So as payment for a debt, he gave it to Penn.

As they did throughout the Americas, Europeans brought new dangers to indigenous peoples. They claimed native lands as their own. Some took what they wanted and didn't hesitate to use force. Even more devastating, they brought with them new diseases like smallpox, influenza, and malaria. These illnesses were troublesome to Europeans. But for indigenous tribes who had no immunity to them, they were almost always deadly. One Lenape chief is quoted as saying, "For every one of you that arrives on a boat, ten of us die."

In the new city of Philadelphia, Penn hoped to create a "holy experiment:" a city of peace and order, unlike any other city in the world. In London, he had experienced crowded, chaotic city streets that seemed to wind in every direction. In Philadelphia, he established a neat grid system for the roads. He had lived through the Great Fire in 1666, which destroyed many of London's tightly packed wooden buildings. In Philadelphia, he required buildings to be made of brick or stone and spaced them out with squares of open land. He had seen Europe's witch trials condemn innocent people. In his court, he intended to rely on reason and mercy, not panic. (In Pennsylvania's one and only witch trial, both defendants were set free by William Penn himself.)

Philadelphia would soon become the second-largest city in the English-speaking world. It was a natural meeting place for another generation with high ideals: the revolutionary thinkers who drafted the Declaration of Independence and the US Constitution. It looked like the city might even become a permanent home for the new national government.

A few years later, though, Philadelphia's fate took a frightening turn. The 1793 yellow fever epidemic swept through the city, killing five thousand people in just a few months. Many more fled, in fear for their lives—including members of the federal government. Though Philadelphians came home when the epidemic passed, the city's role as the nation's capital was at an end. But for Philadelphia's culture and legacy—including landmarks of American history, literary greats like Edgar Allan Poe and *Dracula* author Bram Stoker, exciting true-crime stories, and much more...well, it was only the beginning.

Now you know the official history. Are you ready for some stories too spooky for the history books? Come along on a different kind of tour through Philadelphia. We'll meet dancing ghosts in centuries-old mansions. We'll go inside a haunted prison that still has a hold on long-gone inmates. You'll even learn about the most haunted house in America, right here in Philadelphia. Just turn the page— if you dare!

Carpenter's Hall and the Bank Heist

As you may guess from the name, "Old City" was one of Philadelphia's very first neighborhoods. You might feel like you've gone back in time as you stroll along William Penn's grid-plan streets, lined with stately brick buildings from the 1700s. Watch your step—many of those streets are laid with cobblestones, just as they were when Ben Franklin lived nearby. The cobblestones continue along narrower pathways, too. It's down one of these alleys that you'll spot Old City's Carpenter's Hall. This stately brick building is a fascinating place to admire Georgian architecture, learn about U.S. history . . . and maybe even hear a ghost or two.

Carpenter's Hall was named for the group of craftspeople headquartered there: The Carpenter's Company of the City and County of Philadelphia. The first of these master builders had arrived alongside William Penn back in 1724 and helped build some of the city's most iconic buildings. A century later, their members built Carpenter's Hall and held their first meeting here in 1771.

The structure was large enough to serve multiple uses at a time. Over the years, various groups found a home in Carpenter's Hall. Benjamin Franklin established the Library Company of Philadelphia on the second floor—the first public library in the United States. Later, Franklin—along with George Washington, John Adams, Patrick Henry, and other American founders—held the First Continental Congress here.

In 1798, the Bank of Pennsylvania made its home in the building. A bank vault was added on the basement level, and blacksmith Patrick Lyon was hired to install its new locks. Lyon and his apprentice made and installed the locks as quickly as possible: another yellow fever epidemic was terrorizing Philadelphia, and they were desperate to get out of town. The disease had already killed Lyon's wife and child. He hoped to flee to safety before it infected him, too.

Lyon finished the job and was preparing to leave town when he spotted two men in a tavern, drinking and talking. It was a normal enough scene, but something about the way they were acting struck the blacksmith as suspicious. Lyon recognized one of the pair as Samuel Robinson—the man who had hired him to install the locks. Lyon didn't know the other man, but watching Robinson and the stranger together, he thought to himself, "They are up to no good." Still, there was no time to waste on suspicion now—he had a boat to catch to Delaware. With a sinking feeling, Lyon boarded the vessel with his apprentice and sailed toward safety, leaving the nearly deserted city behind him.

The first piece of bad news was clear on the apprentice's face: The boy had become sick with yellow fever. Shortly after arriving in Delaware, he was dead.

Then, Lyon got more bad news. Just days after he left Philadelphia, the Bank of Philadelphia at Carpenter's Hall had been robbed. The amount stolen was $162,821. That's around three million dollars in today's money! According to reports, there was no sign of forced entry. There was no damage to the new locks. And there was no doubt among the police. This was an inside job . . . and Patrick Lyon was the prime suspect. After all, he had just installed the locks. He knew how to open them. And he had left town . . . right around the time of the theft.

Lyon boarded the ship back toward Philadelphia. With yellow fever still raging in the city, the captain refused to take him all the way there. Lyon went the last thirty miles on foot, determined to clear his name. He was innocent and confident that police would believe his account. Instead of dropping the charges, though, police arrested Lyon and locked him up in the Walnut Street Jail.

There Lyon remained while Isaac Davis, a

member of the Carpenter's Company, made suspiciously large cash deposits in banks all over town. And there he remained when police arrested Davis, and when Davis confessed to robbing the bank with the help of Tom Cunningham, a night porter at Carpenter's Hall. Davis returned the money and was pardoned by the governor, never spending a single hour in jail. But Lyon remained behind bars. For three long months he proclaimed his innocence as he learned of Davis's confession, survived a bout of yellow fever, and appealed to the courts—which at long last set him free.

Lyons wasn't finished fighting for his reputation, though. He sued the bank for false imprisonment and won. He wrote a tell-all book about his time in jail, and commissioned a painting of himself that now hangs in the Pennsylvania Academy of Fine Arts. It would be understandable if he also stuck around in ghostly form, causing a little trouble for the building that had brought so much trouble to him. Many say there is indeed a ghost haunting Carpenter's Hall . . . but it isn't Patrick Lyon.

When Davis confessed to the bank robbery, he didn't take all the blame for himself. He also accused night porter Tom Cunningham. So why wasn't Cunningham charged with a crime? The answer is a grisly one. In the days following the theft, bank employees noticed a dreadful smell wafting through the building. It seemed to be coming from the attic apartments, where Cunningham lived . . . and, as it turned out, where he died. By the time Cunningham's dead body was discovered in his room, it was badly decomposed. Too badly, in fact, to determine a cause of death. It was likely that yellow fever had killed him, so his body was disposed of in haste to avoid further spread of the disease. But was Tom Cunningham a victim of yellow fever? Or did Isaac Davis murder his accomplice to keep him quiet and take his share of the fortune? The mystery remains unsolved.

However his life ended, many say Cunningham's stay in the building never did. In 1960, James and Hazelle O'Connor were living in Carpenter's Hall when they heard loud footsteps in the attic above their bedroom.

They should have been the only ones in the building. They were sure they had been when they locked the front door for the night. The terrified couple called the police and stayed in their room. They were so frightened that when the officers arrived, they dropped the keys down from their window rather than come out to open the door. Before long, the police knocked on the door of their room and told them the coast was clear. "The floor's covered in dust. There are no footprints. No one was up there. Not for a long time, by the look of it," they said. Besides, no one would want to walk around there with the terrible smell that was up there—as if an animal had died. They weren't the first to make this kind of report, the police told the O'Connors, but there was nothing to fear.

After the police left, James and Hazelle walked timidly up the stairs. The footsteps had stopped, but the smell of death was so overpowering they had to turn back. Still a little shaken, they resolved to take a look in the morning and settled down for an uneasy sleep.

When they woke the next day, James and Hazelle felt a little silly about the whole thing. If there was a dead animal in the attic, they would remove the animal and start to clear the air. It would take days for such a strong smell to fade away, but it would over time, they were sure. Together they walked up the stairs again, anticipating the sickly-sweet smell of decay. But as they opened the door, they were amazed to find that the odor had completely disappeared. There was the dusty floor, the empty room, and the smell of old timber—nothing more.

Two nights later, the couple was awakened by footsteps once again. Bolder this time, they opened the door to the hallway. A wall of odor took their breath away. The same sickly smell of death had arrived with the footsteps once again. And again, just as suddenly, the smell was completely gone by morning.

People have encountered a different kind of haunting in the basement, where modern-day tenants do their laundry—and where Davis and Cunningham committed their crime. Some have reported feeling watched by unseen eyes or glimpsing the dark silhouette of a man in the shadows. Down in the laundry room, Hazelle O'Connor once witnessed a chair tip over seemingly on its own. On that occasion, Hazelle fought back nervousness as the family dog whimpered at her side. Determined to finish her task, Hazelle set the chair upright and put the heavy laundry basket on top of it. Then, despite the weight of the heavy basket, the chair tipped over again! The dog growled toward a dark corner, then barked and ran up the stairs. Hazelle wasn't far behind.

Could this be Tom Cunningham, revisiting the fateful scene? Maybe the ghost of Patrick Lyon is trying to ward off intruders...just a couple of hundred years too late. If you're not too spooked by otherworldly energy, stop by Carpenter's Hall next time you're in the neighborhood. You just might come up with a theory of your own. One word of advice, though: If you start to smell something stinky, head for the exits!

City Tavern and the Bonus Bridesmaid

When City Tavern opened in 1773, the Pennsylvania Gazette praised it as being "perfectly in the style of a London tavern." But early patrons at the new restaurant at Walnut and 2nd Street—including Paul Revere, John Adams, and George Washington—would probably have said that City Tavern was proudly American, through and through.

The reasonable prices and delicious food won devoted fans among locals and visitors alike. They stopped to chat over drinks on their way home and celebrated special occasions with feasts of up to 20 courses. Members of the First Continental Congress went to the Tavern frequently to relax after a long day of planning American independence. It became an unofficial headquarters during the Revolutionary War, hosted the first recorded Independence Day party in 1777, and honored the start of George Washington's presidency with an enormous inauguration party at which he was the guest of honor.

The Tavern saw history in the making and held countless amazing memories in its walls. Or at least the *original* Tavern did. After it burned down almost two hundred years ago, a new Tavern was constructed on the same site as the first. Its old-fashioned décor and the servers wearing period costumes are meant to harken back to the original. But the costumes aren't the only part of the past that lingers here. There are said to be two former Philadelphians who still haunt the place today—despite the passage of time, one devastating fire, and even death itself.

One of these ghosts is believed to be a waiter from the Tavern's earliest days. He is said to have been stabbed to death while serving a rowdy party. The murderer, an important military colonel, was never charged. Could the man be back to seek justice on his own terms? Is that him knocking over water glasses and causing plates to crash to the floor with an invisible hand? Some customers even claim to have seen him. They report that a man appears standing in the dining room wearing old-fashioned clothes. In a room full of costumed staff, he blends in at first. But then a small red spot appears on his white shirt. Slowly the spot starts to spread across his chest, as though blood is pouring from his fatal

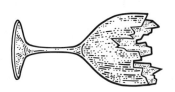

stab wound. Witnesses watch in horror as the man swoons and collapses. As his body reaches the floor, he disappears.

The waiter's story is one of murder, cover-up, and justice denied. It is sad as a story and frightening as a haunting. The Tavern's second ghost leaves a much less straightforward impression, but there is no denying her story is heartbreaking.

It begins full of joy and anticipation: a wedding is to take place right there in the Tavern. The nervous groom is in the bar with his friends, clinking their glasses in a toast to a momentous day. Up a narrow staircase, the bride is dressing for the ceremony surrounded by her bridesmaids. The bridesmaids ooh and ahh over the stunning bride, perhaps admiring how the full-length bridal gown suits her, or how the train of fabric at its back is so luxurious, or how her long brown hair looks even prettier in the candlelight. The room is filled with good friends and warm wishes. Suddenly, a little bit of smoke, a spreading cloud, a terrifying glow. One of the candles must have fallen onto the flowing fabric of the bride's dress! Her friends scream as they crowd around her, trying to douse the flames.

Downstairs, the groom and groomsmen hear the commotion and rush to the staircase. All they can see is smoke. Then a rush of flames as fire engulfs the narrow passageway. There is no possible way to get upstairs. Struggling to breathe, they rush outside to safety. With broken hearts, they watch the building burn as the screams cease: from many, to just a few, and then, finally, silence.

It was a long time before anyone thought to open the Tavern again.

When it did reopen in 1976, anyone who knew this tragic story might have felt a little reluctant to hold their wedding there. But as time passed, the memory of the tragedy faded away, and people began to see again what a happy place this could be for celebrations. And while one ghost seems to like making trouble, the other haunting is kinder, even joyful. These days when bridal parties meet at the Tavern to celebrate, they are kept safe in all kinds of ways. They can flip a switch for light instead of lighting a candle. There are multiple exits to escape any trouble that might arise. There is another safety precaution they might not expect. Sometimes when candles are lit, the flames are mysteriously extinguished—as if someone is making sure the same tragedy doesn't strike twice.

Others don't know they've had a spooky encounter until later. There's a story that repeats with uncanny frequency. It starts much like the story of the doomed wedding from all those years ago. A bride and her bridesmaids are gathered on the second floor, enjoying each other's company as they prepare for the big event. They might be unable to keep a candle lit, but otherwise the celebration seems to go off without a hitch. Only later, while browsing through any pictures taken in the

upstairs room do they see something strange. A picture might show the bride surrounded by her smiling bridesmaids, her oldest and dearest friends. But there is one face in the picture she doesn't recognize: A beautiful young woman with long brown hair, smiling joyfully . . . as joyfully as if this were her own wedding fantasy, coming true at long last.

Powel House: "A Happy Place"

It was October 1965, and a reporter was rushing to yet another interview for her article about "Philadelphia's Haunted Houses—Old and New." So far, Barbara had learned about murders, mayhem, and tragic accidents that were said to have stirred up ghosts in some of the spookiest corners of Philadelphia. With Halloween in the air and sinister spirits in every conversation, she had to admit she was starting to feel a little anxious. She braced for another round of scary stories and rang the doorbell of the redbrick mansion at 244 South Third Street.

What Barbara found at the Powel House was something completely different. Edwin Moore, the historian who lived in the house as caretaker, and his wife, Anne, welcomed her in warmly. Unlike her hosts at other "haunted" houses, these were not jittery witnesses to the paranormal, but two people completely at ease in a house they seemed to love.

Together, the Moores guided Barbara through the home. As they walked, Edwin pointed out the gleaming wood floors and intricate plasterwork and told Barbara about the history of Powel House. It was named, he said, for Samuel and Eliza Powel, who moved here shortly after their marriage in 1769. They were a big deal in Philadelphia society— the heirs of two old, rich families. Well respected in the city, Samuel served terms as mayor both before and after the Revolution. Eliza was quick-witted and well-read, known for her excellent conversation and glittering parties. Together they were an "it" couple. They had famous friends like George and Martha Washington, who held their twentieth-anniversary celebration at Powel House. First Lady Abigail Adams was a particular admirer of Eliza's and a guest at the home. In short, Powel House was the place to be.

Since the 1930s, Powel House had been a historic house museum. During that time, caretakers have lived on-site to look after the place, just like she and her husband did, Anne Moore explained.

It was clear that Edwin and Anne felt warmly connected to the place. They took an interest in its history and looked after it with care and affection. The way they spoke, it seemed like the Moores felt that Powel House took good care of them, too. This was nice, thought Barbara ... but her real goal was to gather some ghost stories and get back to writing her article. She tried to prompt them:

Tell me about a time you felt frightened or anxious here. Do things happen that you can't explain?

The Moores acknowledged that there were some strange happenings in the house, though they never felt ill at ease. "This is a happy place," they concluded. "It always has been."

"Do you believe in ghosts?" asked Barbara.

"No," answered Edwin, "but I don't disbelieve, either."

Barbara Barnes's article was published in the *Philadelphia Bulletin* on October 31, 1965, with these accounts of those "strange happenings." She included this passage with Edwin's report:

> *"One day I was descending the front staircase....I glanced ahead and two young officers were coming up toward me....One wore a blue uniform. He*

looked up and smiled pleasantly. His teeth were very white. Suddenly he was gone."

The Moores are not in the least disturbed by the spirits with whom they apparently share their home . . . . "In the old days, everyone of consequence came here. George Washington, Thomas Jefferson, Benjamin Franklin were frequent visitors." So was the Marquis de Lafayette. And Moore feels it may have been he who was ascending the staircase.

Anne Moore told the reporter about a ghostly figure she calls "my pretty lady" and the lively social scene that somehow echoes still at Powel House:

"She was fanning and tapping her foot,"

the historian's wife recalls. "Her black hair was piled high with pearls. Her dress was beige and lavender. She looked directly at me. When I snapped on the light, the chair where she had been was empty."

> "...sometimes if you turn the light on suddenly in the big drawing room, the whole floor squeaks as if a lot of people were hurriedly leaving."

Edwin Moore spent 16 years working at Powel House. He has since passed away, but some think he still sometimes visits the place where he felt so happy...just to make sure things are running as they should. Site managers who came after the Moores report feeling

watched while they tend to the house—never in a threatening way, but rather as though someone is checking over the quality of their work. There have been times when a site manager has turned off lights and they've turned themselves back on. Alarms have gone off seemingly on their own.

Powel House might not be at capacity yet. When historian Mickey Herr moved into Powel House, she brought along a pet: a skinny black and white cat named Maggie Mae. Maggie had always been nervous and shy. Now, to

Mickey's surprise, the cat took to the house in a heartwarming way, becoming calmer and more confident while she lived there for the remainder of her days. A couple of years after Maggie died, one of the home's historians reported chasing a skinny black and white cat through the house, only to have it disappear. Mickey was sure she knew just who it was.

If you visit Powel House, keep an eye out for Edwin and Maggie Mae. If you love it there as much as they do, they just might let you stay.

Don't Forget about Joseph Fry!

When it comes to major moments in American history, one building has hosted more than its fair share: Philadelphia's Pennsylvania State House—or, as it's now called, Independence Hall. The name tells you something about its history. The founders and framers met here to discuss their grievances under English rule, and later to declare independence from the monarchy. A first attempt at a constitution (the

Articles of Confederation) was written here, as well as the US Constitution we know today. The founding ideals of our country were debated within these walls by George Washington, Benjamin Franklin, Thomas Jefferson, John Adams, Alexander Hamilton, James Madison, and more.

The Pennsylvania State House wasn't just the home of America's founding documents. Until the year 1800, it was also the home of the new American government. The Supreme Court, Senate, and House of Representatives were all based in this very building. The president was based just one block away. Some of the most powerful people in the world

have spent time here—people with big ideas and big voices; people accustomed to being center-stage, who weren't afraid to let their presence be felt. Is it any wonder some of them are still hanging around the place where they made so much history?

That shadowy figure walking the halls at night, seemingly deep in thought—could it be Ben Franklin? Or perhaps it's Abraham Lincoln, who stopped here when he was on his way to Washington to be sworn in as president. The next time he was here was after his assassination—his coffin was displayed here during his nationwide funeral procession. But was it the last time?

Assembly Hall once rang loud with impassioned speeches about democracy and debates about what form the new government should take. Could those distant echoes

explain the voices security guards sometimes hear late at night from the empty hall?

Not every chapter in Independence Hall's past has been quite so noble. During the Revolution, British soldiers occupied the building. They kept prisoners of war in a second-floor "hospital" that became known for its terrible conditions. Those who survived reported being fed meager rations or nothing at all. Those who died were cast into a mass grave. It may be one of those suffering soldiers who has been heard coughing on the second floor, and calling weakly, "Help me!"

After the war, Philadelphians faced a different kind of enemy: yellow fever. Members of the new US government, still based in the State House, monitored the situation nervously. It would be a disaster for the new country if all its leaders suddenly fell ill—or worse. However, the infection seemed confined to a different part of town. It seemed possible that it wouldn't come near the building.

During those years, Joseph Fry worked as a guard in the State House and lived in one of its small apartments. On August 29, 1793, Joseph's dead body was found there with signs indicating he'd died of yellow fever. Government officials and their staff had already fled the city in terror. Either no one was there to move Joseph's body or they didn't dare move or bury him. Either way, his body remained in the apartment for many weeks. When people returned to the city, Joseph's

remains were buried in a mass grave. However, that might have been too little, too late for the restless spirit of Joseph Fry, as two guards discovered hundreds of years later.

Independence Hall was closed and locked as the guards kept watch. All was quiet, as usual until a voice from headquarters came over their radios with an alert: an alarm had been tripped. The sensors detected an intruder in the building! The guards rushed to the site of the alarm, but there was no one in sight. They radioed back to headquarters: "We searched the whole building. No signs of an intruder." It must have been a false alarm.

When the radio sounded again, however, the voice from headquarters sounded even more alarmed: "There's definitely a man in the building. We saw him on camera for a second, but the feed must have cut out. No doors have been opened. He's in there somewhere."

So the guards looked again, searching every corner. "We're not finding anyone," they reported. "If you see him again let us know where—we'll go there right away."

There was quiet while the dispatcher seemed to be checking different rooms on the video feed. Then the dispatcher gasped and told the guards, "I do see him—he's standing beside you!"

The guards looked quickly around the room. Nothing was out of place ... but as they looked at an empty staircase, they both heard the sound of footsteps. As the steps grew louder, a man in colonial clothes seemed to materialize out of thin air. He staggered down the stairs toward them, getting closer every second. The guards raced out of the building. And unlike the staffers who fled yellow fever all those years ago, these two never returned.

Grave Robbers, Doctors, and Ghosts

Just a block away from Independence Hall is a public square where Philadelphians love to picnic, stroll, and play. Today, it's known as Washington Square. It's full of life. But back when it was known as Southeast Square, it was better known as a place for the dead.

Southeast Square was originally designed by William Penn, who probably envisioned it being used as it is today. In the 1700s, though, it was used as a burying ground. This was a century marked by deadly epidemics and war. Philadelphia had more dead bodies than it could handle. Sometimes families buried their departed loved ones in graves here in the square. At other times this was a "potter's field"—a place where enormous twenty-by-thirty-foot holes were dug as mass

graves. When people died and their families couldn't afford a burial, or when sickness or war meant burials had to happen fast and cheap, bodies were wrapped in canvas and piled high here. When a hole filled up, the grave keepers would cover it with dirt and start a new one. With no markers or tombstones to indicate who was in the mass graves, people began to refer to this area as "Strangers Burying Ground." During the American Revolution alone, thousands of soldiers were among the strangers buried there. In 1793, the yellow fever epidemic killed 5,000 more in the city, many of whom were buried here.

In addition to victims of illness and war, Strangers Burying Ground served another community: enslaved people and free people of color. Racist practices prevented them from being buried in most church cemeteries, so some dug graves for their loved ones in the park. Many free people of color lived in the homes surrounding the park. Burying their dead there meant they could stay close to this sacred space while also providing some protection for the gravesites.

Protecting the graves was no small feat. There were those who wanted to take what was in the coffins: not jewelry or riches, but the bodies. Dissecting the recently deceased was one way doctors learned about the human body in those days. There were no X-rays or MRIs, so if a doctor wanted to find out what the muscles

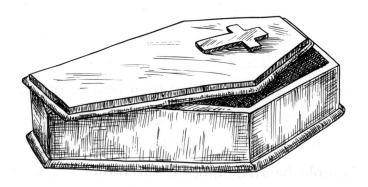

and organs of human bodies really looked like, they cut some bodies open to look. There was no legal way to acquire the bodies for this practice. There was, however, a community of criminals that was only too happy to provide them, for a fee.

The gruesome practice was always more or less the same. Grave robbers would search the cemetery for a fresh grave, then dig up the coffin, remove the body, and deliver it to the doctor. Richard Allen and Absalom Jones, leaders of black churches nearby, were among those who asked the government to help stop the graverobbers by building a wall around the area where their church members were buried. They were ignored. Instead, ordinary citizens took up the cause, doing their best to protect fresh graves and keep the grave robbers away.

One of these guardians was Leah, a "simple-hearted innocent," according to one of her contemporaries. The writer, John Fanning Watson, described Leah like this:

> *"Leah, a half-crazed, specter-looking, elderly maiden lady, tall and thin, of the Society of Friends. Among her oddities, she sometimes used to pass the night, wrapped in a blanket, between the graves at this place, for the avowed purpose of frightening away the doctors!"*

Leah was dedicated to her mission, even sleeping in the graveyard to protect the dead.

In fact, she kept up her nightly watch until the day she joined them. Leah was found one early morning, lying on a grave she had been protecting. The person in that grave may be resting easier thanks to Leah's efforts, along with an untold number of others she watched over. There are others, perhaps those whom Leah just couldn't protect, who are anything but restful.

In 1794, Strangers Burying Ground was closed. There was simply no more room. With no fresh graves, the threat of grave robbers had passed. Since then, the park has been beautified with trees and plants. Now, you can

go to Washington Square to look at the lovely plantings, take a walk along the pathways, or rest under a shady tree on a sunny day. Just be warned: visitors just like you have seen more than they planned for.

People walking through the park at night have caught glimpses of Revolutionary War soldiers in bloody uniforms, their ghostly forms hovering above the ground while their bones lie beneath it. Other visitors spot victims of yellow fever. Their funeral rites would have been especially hurried since it was mistakenly believed that even a dead body could spread infection. More than any other ghost, however, people report seeing a tall old woman, dressed in an old-fashioned black dress, a black cloak, and a frayed blanket around her shoulders. She sometimes appears in photographs. People see her standing right in front of them: frail and stooped, perhaps tired from her efforts in this very park during its days as a graveyard, perhaps watching still, to help its residents rest easy. As for Leah herself—she doesn't seem ready to rest easy quite yet.

Eastern State: A Short Story of a Long Incarceration

Eastern State Penitentiary is full of contradictions. Despite its fortress-like façade, designed to intimidate, it goes by the sweet-sounding nickname "Cherry Hill." When it was opened in 1829, it was considered modern and progressive. At the time, Philadelphians were accustomed to the infamous Walnut Street Jail—a small, unsanitary place where prisoners got into just as much trouble (or more) behind bars as they had outside. The jailers were corrupt, too, always looking for a way to make money off the people in their charge and allowing violence to reign among them. Disease spread easily in the tight quarters, and the putrid air outside didn't help, especially during yellow fever outbreaks, when mass graves nearby filled with decomposing bodies.

Eastern State was meant to change all that with a system designed for health, solitude, and reflection. Walnut Street Jail aimed only to punish, but Eastern State was about reform. Even the design of the building was meant to encourage people to search their souls, repent for their crimes, and find a better path. The vaulted ceilings looked almost like a church. Reading material was limited, but you could ask for a Bible. For human contact, options included a daily chat with the warden or a visit with the chaplain. Otherwise, activities were limited to exercise or wholesome work, such as carving or shoemaking. The atmosphere was quiet, with every prisoner assigned his or her own room with its own attached exercise yard—unlike the crowded, noisy chaos of Walnut Street Jail. Eastern State even had a flush toilet in every cell, boasting full indoor plumbing before even the White House. Its approach was revolutionary and set a standard for hundreds of prisons after it. The last inmate left the Penitentiary in 1971. But there are signs that some of its prisoners never really left.

These days, Eastern State Penitentiary is a tourist attraction, operating as a museum year-round. Around Halloween, it hosts a popular haunted house. For the occasion, local actors are positioned at various stations throughout the cell blocks, playing the role of prisoners and trying to spook visitors. Some of those actors return year after year, and they figure out which stations are all in good fun ... and which are a little *too* spooky for comfort. One cell block might be completely peaceful, while in another the actors hear hushed voices or shuffling footsteps. Still other blocks echo with haunting screams, scaring the actors as much as they hope to scare the visitors!

If you ever have a chance to work at the museum or haunted house, think twice before you say yes ... or at least ask which cell block you'd be working in. Block 6? If you're not easy to scare, it might be OK. You are likely to hear people talking or moving nearby, but if you approach them, you'll hear them hurrying away from you. The strange thing is, you'll never see them. Block 4? It depends on how brave you're feeling—you're likely to hear sounds,

but you may also see the ghost of a prisoner. (A ghost prisoner was even caught on film there once!) Block 12? You might want to turn down that assignment. One haunted house manager didn't believe it when an actor who was stationed in Block 12 reported a screaming woman running toward him, then turning to run screaming in the other direction, and then vanishing. A few years later, she heard the exact same story from a different actor, who claimed, "It was like a banshee!" Then she believed!

Eastern State is well worth a visit. It's a fascinating look at a different side of history. If you do decide to go, just remember 4, 6, and 12 are the most haunted blocks. If you love a good scare, you'll want to head right to them. If not, steer clear!

Lost at Fort Mifflin

Where the Delaware and Schuylkill Rivers meet, there's an old army fort on Mud Island. As you may guess from the island's name, this may not be the place you'd choose to build your dream house. Especially in summer, its swampy surroundings featured a boggy odor and lots of mosquitoes. For a fort to protect the city of Philadelphia, however, the location was perfect. The timing wasn't bad either.

Construction of the new fort finished in 1776—just in time to play a role in the American Revolution. Washington's army had suffered defeat at the Battle of Brandywine. With 250 British ships on the way to Philadelphia, there was little time for General Washington to regroup and reposition for the next encounter. The 400 Patriots on Mud Island were too few to stop the 1,000 enemy troops, but they fought valiantly enough that Washington could retreat to safety and fight another day. The Fort was nearly destroyed during the Battle of Mud Island, but after the war it was rebuilt and renamed for Thomas Mifflin, the first governor of Pennsylvania.

During the Civil War, the fort was a prison—not just for captured Confederate soldiers, but for Union soldiers who violated military rules, and some civilians, too. Punishments were harsh and conditions were poor. During the winter, broken windows let in punishing cold air. In the summer, mosquitoes spread diseases like typhoid and dysentery. Many died from illness, overcrowding, or lack of food and water.

During World War I and World War II, Fort Mifflin served as an ammunition supply depot for the US Navy. Then, in 1954, it was decommissioned (released from military service). In its next phase, there was less live ammunition and more visitors coming to the island ... or at least more visitors *leaving* the island ....

Soon after Fort Mifflin opened as a historic site, people began to notice odd happenings. The sound of metalwork was heard coming from the old blacksmith shop, though no one was inside. People would tell each other about a "reenactor" in a Confederate uniform, who sat cleaning his gun while he shared stories about the past in amazing detail—only to learn that none of the reenactors on the island were wearing Confederate uniforms that day. Other ghosts appeared in less detail—just shadows crouching in the corner of a cell or dart across a hallway as if trying to hide from view.

There are two ghosts, however, who seem to have very clear identities: William Howe and Elizabeth Pratt. Most people just call them by their chilling aliases: "the Faceless Man" and "the Screaming Lady."

Private William Howe fought for the Union Army during the Civil War. He became known for his skill with a rifle, which earned him the respect of his peers. Things were going well for William, right up until he became sick with dysentery. Unfortunately, the military hospital was full and could not help him. William knew he needed treatment fast—dysentery was a common cause of death in those days.

Desperate, he went home to find a doctor who would treat him. In time, he was cured. By the military's standards, though, he was also now guilty of desertion. Three officers showed up at William's home, ready to arrest him. Hoping to scare them away, he grabbed his rifle and fired a shot in their direction. He didn't mean to hit anyone . . . but before he knew it, he had bigger problems than desertion. One of the officers was dead, and William was under arrest for desertion *and* murder.

William Howe was tried, found guilty, and sentenced to death by hanging. While the gallows were built for his execution—the first and only execution at Fort Mifflin—he was imprisoned in the fort's casemate (a fortress room) #11. The wall still bears his signature today. But that's not the only sign of William on Mud Island: A man in a Union army uniform might not stand out in a place with historical exhibits. When people come across the man looking sorrowfully down at the ground near the entrance to the casemates, though, they know there is something strange in his appearance. At first, they can't tell what is off. But as they come closer, the man turns toward them, and they see. He doesn't have a face! It may be a shadow of his final moments, when a black hood was placed over his head just before the noose tightened around his neck.

You are more likely to hear Elizabeth Pratt than to see her. That was true for the neighbors who called the police to report someone being attacked when they heard her desperate cries. In truth, Elizabeth's terror was not violence, but sadness. Elizabeth's husband was stationed at Fort Mifflin and she and their daughter lived there with him. Then, in 1802, the family welcomed their second child: a son. All we know of the two children, sadly, is what was in the records of the island's cemetery. In July of that year, the baby died. In December, the daughter died, too. Their heartbroken mother surely wailed with grief at so great a loss. Within a few short months, she too was dead. Yellow fever was likely the cause of all three deaths, since it was so common during those years. Mud Island's mosquitoes would have made it even easier to become infected. It is easy to imagine, though, that Elizabeth died from heartache. You may feel it too, if you hear her desperate cry. What may be even sadder is another ghost connected to her story. Some visitors have come across a little girl wandering alone, looking lost and upset. When people ask her what is wrong, she answers, "Looking for Mommy..." and then disappears.

CHAPTER
8

Baleroy Mansion: A Crowded House

Judith Haines took a step into Baleroy Mansion, a 32-room estate in Philadelphia's lovely Chestnut Hill neighborhood. Judith, a trained psychic, was always looking for signs of otherworldly activity. If anyone was going to pick up on a ghostly presence, it was her. But even Judith was amazed at the level of activity at Baleroy. Almost without meaning to she exclaimed, "I can't believe how many spirits are in this house!"

George Easby, on the other hand, was taught *not* to believe in ghosts. While living at Baleroy, George's father tried hard to convince him that there was nothing spooky behind things like a loud crash that seemed to come from nowhere, or creaking sounds in the night, or the framed picture that seemed to fly off the wall and fall onto the floor. Of course, all the strange things that seemed to happen at Baleroy made it hard for George to take his father's lesson to heart.

The Easby family moved into Baleroy Mansion in 1926, when George was eight years old and his little brother, Stevey, was six. Soon after they moved in, the two boys went outside to explore. When they came across a fountain, the boys peered into the water. George saw his own face reflected on the water's surface . . . but as he peered over to where Stevey's reflection should be, he did not see his brother's fresh face and blond hair. The reflection showed not a face, but a skull! Not long after that, little Stevey died of an illness. Perhaps the skeleton had been a sign of his fate . . . or perhaps it was a sign that Stevey already had a connection to the world of the dead. He would certainly prove later that he still had a connection to the world of the living. Soon after Stevey's funeral, George saw his little brother appear in the room where he had died. Since then, many others have seen it too—sometimes from outside the house, where a face in the window shows the young boy's face.

Built in 1911, Baleroy is not as old as many of the locations in this book (though the Easby family who lived there for decades came to Philadelphia on William Penn's ship, way back in 1683). It's not the most famous—a distinction that goes to Philadelphia's top tourist sites. It does, however, have one very spooky distinction: "the most haunted house in America." Baleroy doesn't just have a lot of paranormal activity . . . it has a lot of *kinds* of paranormal activity. For instance, there are ghosts like Stevey. There are phantom sounds like the sound of a car driving by when nothing is there. There is the persistent feeling of being watched . . . even for those just passing by on the sidewalk. Objects move on their own—like a painting flinging itself off the wall and onto the floor, a recording device yanked out of one visitor's hands, or a copper pot speeding through the air toward a visitor's head. There is a bluish blob of supernatural energy that hangs in the air. Objects seem to be haunted by their past. Ghost monks give business advice. ("No, Mr. Easby, No!" one shouted at a time George Easby was deciding whether or not to make an investment, saving him from financial disaster.)

George Easby took all of this in stride. Asked what it was like to grow up in a haunted house, George said casually, "Occasionally I would see a figure in the room when it wasn't there. You'd hear people going up the stairs when no one was here. Things like that." To a friend who looked a little spooked after passing the room that Stevey haunted, George simply said, "You must have seen my brother." When a visitor was spooked by a glowing, floating blob in the extra-haunted Blue Room, George explained, "Oh, that's just the ectoplasm."

George's parents seemed equally at ease in the house. (George's father never acknowledged the haunting while he lived there, though.) George's mother, Henrietta, seemed to know every corner. Even in her later years, when she needed a cane to walk, her steps could be heard through the house as her cane thumped the beat of her progress. One of Henrietta's favorite rooms was the library, where she could sit and read Longfellow's "The Children's Hour"—her favorite poem. Henrietta died in 1962 . . . but even after her death, the sound of her cane sometimes echoed in an upstairs hallway.

Seven years later, George's father died as well. George was his parents' heir, so when his father died George received ownership of the house and its contents. He also found a letter left for him by his father. In it, his father finally acknowledged that there were ghosts at Baleroy after all. (It's safe to say that George had that pretty well figured out by this point.) His father also told George that Henrietta was one of the ghosts he'd seen, appearing to stand beside his bed twice after her death.

Among the items George inherited with the house was a priceless collection of antiques. There was a clock that belonged to French

queen Marie Antoinette. The pistol, desk, and dining table were from George's ancestor General George Meade, who led the Union Army to victory in the Battle of Gettysburg during the Civil War. An oil lamp had been excavated from the ruins of Pompeii (an ancient city that was frozen in time when a volcano erupted in the year 79 CE). It was truly a museum's worth of treasures, most with fascinating connections to history. So, George hired a curator and began finding ways to share them with more people. They sent items from "the Baleroy Collection" on loan to the Philadelphia Museum of Art, the Metropolitan Museum of Art, and the White House.

Not every piece in the house was good for sharing, though. There was one chair that visitors were discouraged from trying.

It was a lovely wingback chair, upholstered in blue, that had belonged to French Emperor Napoleon Bonaparte at one time. At Baleroy, its home was the Blue Room, which was thought to be the home's most haunted location. But even in that spooky space, the "Death Chair" stood out as especially sinister. George Easby wasn't sure about the source of the rumors that it had been made originally by a warlock. But when it came to the other legend—that sitting in the chair would mark a person for death—there was no denying the frightening truth. Four people are known to have died soon after sitting in the chair.

Paul Kimmons was a curator who helped care for the collection. Unlike George, Paul spent years at Baleroy without a single supernatural experience. When George told him about Amanda, one of Baleroy's most active ghosts,

Paul just chuckled. He didn't believe in ghosts, and he wasn't going to start now ... or so he thought.

One day, Paul was giving a tour when he saw a ghostly woman walking down the stairs. He felt a chill run up his spine but tried to put the encounter out of his mind. It turned out Amanda had other ideas. Paul started seeing Amanda everywhere: in his car, in his bedroom at home, on the sidewalk. Weeks went by and Paul was really starting to think he was losing his mind. It didn't help that he was trying to keep the odd happenings to himself. After all, he had teased George for years about being superstitious. But Paul was exhausted from lack of sleep, frightened by Amanda's appearances, and more and more jumpy. He started to expect the ghostly face to spring out from around every corner.

So, Paul arrived at Baleroy one day and

began to tell George the whole story. In his exhaustion, he was barely paying attention to where he was. Paul sunk into a nearby chair as he spoke. Not just any chair—the Death Chair! George later put a rope over the chair's arms to keep people from sitting in it. But it was too late for Paul, who died soon after, becoming #4 on the Death Chair's list of victims.

When the psychic Judith Haines first visited Baleroy, she was amazed by the number of spirits. Over time, she got used to the ghosts she met there, and they got used to her, too. Perhaps that's why George's deceased mother chose Judith to help her communicate with her son. Henrietta, who had known so much about the house and its contents, seemed to want to share some valuable information with her son. Judith received Henrietta's messages from beyond and passed them along to George. First, George was guided to a dusty corner of the attic, where he found a pair of antique silver candlesticks that his mother had stored there decades before. Next, he was directed to a cabinet in the Blue Room, where some old legal documents had been stored and then forgotten. When George read them, he learned that he had rights to an additional inheritance—a fortune that he'd never heard of now belonged to him.

On another visit, Judith reported that on her way to the house she had heard one word from the spirit world: Longfellow. Did that mean anything to George? George knew immediately where this clue was leading him. He walked

straight to the library to look for his mother's favorite book. He didn't have to look very hard. The books were stored in neat rows along the shelves, their old leather spines all aligned with one another. All except one. George pulled out the book: a collection of poems by Henry Wadsworth Longfellow. It opened to his mother's favorite poem, "The Children's Hour," and an empty envelope on which was written, "To my son . . . in the event of my death."

It could be that the envelope once held directions to the treasures that Judith helped George to find. It is possible that there were more riches that the contents would have helped uncover. What had been in the envelope, and who had taken it? That is a mystery for another day.

Baleroy was sold after George's death. The contents were relocated to museums around the world, and a new family moved into the house. It's possible that as they settled into the house, they met the same collection of ghosts familiar to the Easby family. It's also possible there was a new cast of characters as the spirits connected

with objects moved to their new homes. Did Amanda depart at last when the Death Chair was carried away? Did Henrietta and Stevey finally rest once the last of their family was gone? Or, perhaps, did George join them in wandering the halls and gazing out the windows of the home he loved so much? During his lifetime, he certainly didn't rule it out: "When I leave here, I'm coming back to haunt them, he said. "If they don't take good care of this place I'm going to be right back here after them."

CHAPTER 9

A Famous Name, a Forgotten Woman

Philadelphians are proud of their city's important role in American history, and of the impressive people that have shaped it. Some of those people have become central figures in history books, starring in stories that Philly's citizens are glad to share. Some have made a name in sports, entertainment, or art. Some very wealthy people have found another way to lasting fame: sharing their wealth with schools and other institutions, which in turn bear the names of their benefactors. One of these rich patrons was Stephen Girard.

Stephen Girard didn't start out rich. He was born in France in 1750, the son of a sailor. His beginnings were humble, but young Stephen had big goals. So, he moved to Philadelphia in 1776, seeking opportunity. Right away his dreams seemed to take hold: He met a beautiful young woman named Mary, fell in love, and married her. Then his grocery business took off, and his fortune began to grow. By the time he died, Stephen Girard would be the richest person in the United States. Stephen's money bought him a life of great luxury. It also made him powerful. Nobody said "no" to Stephen Girard. He could pretty much do whatever he wanted.

These days, people who know the name "Girard" are usually connected to the school named after him. That's how Charlie Roseman and Bob Ross knew the name over one hundred years later: as graduates of Girard College.

One day, while sharing stories about their college days, Charlie, Bob, and their friend Joe Vendetti became curious about the story behind the name. When Joe retired and had some free time, he started researching. He learned of Stephen's background and work, about his vast fortune and sizeable donations— sizeable enough to have his name on "Girard College" and earn him a prominent plaque on the first floor of Pennsylvania Hospital. But when it came to Mrs. Girard, it was hard to find anything at all. Joe knew that women's writings and life stories from the era would have been considered less important than men's, so he wasn't surprised that the records weren't voluminous. But there were no letters, no diaries, no portraits . . . in fact, there was so very little recorded about her, Joe thought, it was almost as if she'd disappeared. As Joe read through Stephen's writings, pieces of the story began to come together. With surprise and sadness, Joe realized that "disappeared" wasn't so far from the truth. Here's what he learned.

In 1758, Mary Lum was born in Philadelphia, the daughter of a shipbuilder. Dark-haired and beautiful, Mary had just turned 18 when everything she knew seemed to change: Not far from her home, men were writing the Declaration of Independence, about to transform the country and its future. Around the same time, Mary met Stephen Girard and fell in love. She married him a year later.

In the beginning, the Girards were happy newlyweds. For eight years or so, they lived in luxury and relative peace. Then Mary began to suffer from mental illness. Around age twenty-seven, she started acting differently—flying into wild rages or falling into deep sadness. Often, she was unable to contain her emotions or control her actions.

Stephen wrote to his brother, "It is not a physical ailment, it is of the mind.... The illness of this virtuous woman has so unsettled my life." He seemed mostly concerned about his own peace of mind. But at least he described Mary with a bit of kindness. After two years, recovery was seeming less and less likely, and Stephen was growing more and more cruel. Instead of a "virtuous woman," letters to his brother call her an "unfortunate vixen." He decided that his marriage was basically over (though legally it was not)... and he started to act as though Mary weren't even there. He even moved another woman into the house to fill Mary's role as a loving partner, ignoring his wife's distress. After two years of this unhappy arrangement, he was planning to take it even further: moving Mary out of the house completely and confining her to a hospital. There was only one facility that would take her. Wouldn't you know, it was Pennsylvania Hospital—the one that had Stephen's name on a plaque on the wall. Would they deny any request from this rich and powerful man? It didn't look like it.

In 1790, Stephen had Mary committed to Pennsylvania Hospital as an "incurable lunatic." She had a comfortable room and some extra privileges, but in essence, she was imprisoned. She would never leave the grounds again. Mary Lum Girard remained confined there for twenty-five years, until her death in 1815.

Her cause of death is not recorded. Stephen attended the private funeral on the hospital grounds, and a written record describes his behavior as affectionate and sad, with a tear rolling down his cheek and glistening on his dead wife's face as he tenderly bid her farewell. There's reason to believe, though, that the details of this report of Mary's funeral were somewhat unreliable . . . especially the warmth of Stephen's goodbye, expressed in a tender tear. This would have been very hard for the witness to see, since the burial was held in the dark of night, probably to avoid being noticed. Like so much of her life, Mary's death was shrouded in secrecy and shame. At Stephen's request, her body was buried in an unmarked grave, dug into the north lawn of the hospital grounds.

Would it surprise you to hear that Mary now haunts the hospital where her sad life ended?

People staying in the room where she died say they have seen her in the middle of the night, standing at the foot of their beds. Others have spotted a ghostly figure in a white dress walking across the northern lawn, toward the very spot where Mary was buried. People think this must be her—though with so few records

of her appearance, it is impossible to know if the ghost resembles her. We don't know what Mary looked like, but we can certainly guess at her sadness. When people hear a woman's heartbreaking crying near where Mary's room was located, they wonder if it's her ghost. Stephen Girard may or may not have cried at her funeral, but Mary certainly shed many tears during the unhappy later years of her life. Perhaps she is still crying now.

It seems Stephen's spirit is restless, as well. He was buried in the cemetery of Holy Trinity Church, not far from the hospital. His body was later moved to a memorial on the grounds of Girard College ... but his ghost is said to haunt the cemetery still today.

Joe Vendetti shared all of this with Charlie and Bob, and the three friends agreed that something needed to be done. It was no wonder that Mary couldn't rest peacefully after such a lonely end! It was a final injustice that Stephen Girard had been buried twice—with two ceremonies and two marked gravesites— when Mary had none. Perhaps they could help

her. Together, Joe, Charlie, and Bob paid for a tombstone to mark Mary's grave properly, and finally bring her some recognition and peace. When they presented it to Pennsylvania Hospital, however, the hospital refused to accept it. So, the gravesite is still unmarked, its story untold. And Mary Lum wanders on, making her presence known in death as it never was in life.

A Ghostly Goodbye from the City of Brotherly Love

Would you dare to visit these spooky Philly sites? They're well worth the time—*if* you like hearing unexplained noises, spotting eerie shadows, and spotting the occasional ghost. Just bring a bit of courage (and maybe a flashlight!) and you'll *probably* emerge without a copper pot flying toward you.

When you walk out of their doors, don't let your guard down—remember, wherever there is a little bit of history, there may be spirits hanging around to relive it. And if any place has a lot of history, it's spooky Philadelphia!

Beth Hester spent her childhood in the haunted city of New Orleans, where she sometimes heard ghostly footsteps in the very old house where she lived . . . and awoke one morning to find a mysterious footprint on her ceiling! These days, she lives in New England with her husband, their two children, and one spooky dog, and (most of) the footprints stay on the floor. You can find her at bethhester.com.

Check out some of the other *Spooky America* titles available now!

Spooky America was adapted from the creeptastic *Haunted America* series for adults. *Haunted America* explores historical haunts in cities and regions across America. Here's more from the original *Haunted History of Philadelphia* author, Josh Hitchens:

www.joshhitchens.com

Books by Jinx Schwartz

The Hetta Coffey series

Just Add Water, Book 1
Just Add Salt, Book 2
Just Add Trouble, Book 3
Just Deserts, Book 4
Just the Pits, Book 5
Just Needs Killin', Book 6

The Hetta Coffey Boxed Set, Books 1-4

Troubled Sea
The Texicans
Land Of Mountains

JUST NEEDS KILLIN'
by
Jinx Schwartz